Just a Few Feathers

poems for the seasons of life by

Ute Carson

Plain View Press
P.O. 42255
Austin, TX 78704

plainviewpress.net
pk@plainviewpress.net
512-441-2452

ISBN: 978-1-935514-00-8
Library of Congress Number: 2011925678

Cover art: *Feather Collage* by Brenda Marks
Cover design by Pam Knight

This book is dedicated

to my grandchildren

Acknowledgements

Gratitude to the folowing publications for publishing the poems below.
"The Wound" and "Expectations," *Arts & Letters Magazine*, Summer issue 2005; "Despair," *The Barricade*, a political poetry ezine, December 2005; "Moving to the Condo" and "The Stones Concert 2005," *The Texas Observer*, June 2006; "Bliss," *The WriterWithin*, August 2006; "Mother Love," Placed in *The Secret Attic Poetry Competition*, June 2006; "Sorry," *The Jimson Journal*, September 2006; "Beyond US" and "Naturalization," *Timbuktu*, online magazine, UK, 2006; "Marriage," *AWEN* # 47, August 2007; "Stirring," Third Place in the Eugene Walter Writers' Festival Vivian Smallwood Poetry Competition, October 2006. No publication; "Stirring" and "Imperfection," *Reese Taylor Award in Poetry*, Inkpot Press, Volume 2007; "First Arrival" December 2006, "Grief" June 2007, and "Tender Aging" and "Our Time" in August 2007, *Decanto* by Masque Publishing (UK); "The Birth of a Poem" Issue 24 August 2007, and "Goodnight Moon" Issue 25 November 2007, *Earth Love Magazine*, *Poetry for the Environment*; "Song of Autumn," First Place Free Verse Poem in *Lyrical Passion*, April 2007; "White Feathers," Poet of Distinction Award from Florence Poets Society in *Silkworm*, 2007; "Artifacts," *Illya's Honey*, Dallas Poets Community, Vol.13, Fall/Winter 2007; "Success," Second Place Winner in *The Blind Man's Rainbow Journal of Poetry & Art*, Blind Press, Volume XII, Issue 1, Winter 2007; "I Will Still Miss the Yearning," Texas Senior Lauriat Honor Scroll Award 2007 from Amy Kitchener's Angels Without Wings Foundation, Inc. No publication; "Recognition," *Wild Things Domestic and Otherwise*, Edited by Whitney Scott, Outrider Press, Inc., 2008; "Holding On For Dear Life," "In the Face of Death," "Permanence in Change," and "The Gift," *Literary Magic*, Fall Issue 2008; "Hit the Road," "Inner Light," and "Put a Kiss on a Wish," *Free Xpression*, Australia, Vol. XVI, Issue I, 2009; "Sickbed," *Shots*, UK, Edition 3, 2009; "Mummum's Lebanese Meat Pies," *Dreamcatcher*, The Laurel Crown Foundation, San Antonio, 2009; EXSE Spoken Word Showcase 2009, produced in honor of National Poetry Month. I was chosen to read several poems on ChannelAustin, Austin, TX; "Transformation," Award of Merit 2009 from the League of Minnesota Poets. No publication; "After the First There is No Other" & "Birthday Omen," *Audience*, World Audience Publishers, Vol. 4, No. 2, Fall 2009; EXSE Spoken Word Showcase 2010, produced in honor of National Poetry Month. I read several poems on ChannelAustin, TX; "A Colorful Well-Worn Garment," ARDENT, A Journal of Poetry & Art, Vol.5:1, 2010.

Contents: *Just a Few Feathers*

Spring   7

Success	9
Bliss	10
First Arrival	11
Our Time	12
Expectations	13
Mother Love	14
Inner Light	15
Birthday Omen	16
Mother's Day	17
Gratitude	18
Transformation	19
My Garden	20
In Praise of My Mother's Womb	21
Lifeline	22
Ode to My Thumb	23

Summer Then Fall   25

Driftwood	27
Dread	28
No Change	29
Loneliness	30
Me	31
You and Me	32
The Gift	33
Imperfection	34
The Loner	35
Temptation	36
Hit the Road	37
At the Funeral	38
Despair	39
Asking Forgiveness From the Dead	40
Song of Autumn	41
Recognition	42
Naturalization	43
Dreams of Fame	44
Acceptance	45
Festival of Lights	46
Mummum's Lebanese Meat Pies	47
Sickbed	48
What Remains	49

Artifacts 50

Staying the Course 51

Winter 53

White Feathers 55

Moving to the Condo 56

The Old Woman 57

Stirring 58

Tender Aging 59

Permanence in Change 60

How Careless We Were 61

Preparing For a Colonoscopy 62

I Will Still Miss the Yearning 63

Stones Concert 2005 64

In the Face of Death 65

Absent Fathers 67

Photographs 68

Waiting 69

Holding on For Dear Life 70

A Colorful Well-Worn Garment 71

Loose Feathers 73

Beyond Us 75

Thank Goodness 76

Never Just Sex 77

Sweet Dreams For a Newborn 78

Put a Kiss on a Wish 79

Only in My Dreams 80

Butterfly 81

Letztes Geleit — Final Escort 82

Retrieval 83

Wisdom 84

Buddha Belly 85

Love's Embrace 86

There But For the Grace of God Go I 87

Ordinary Lives 88

The Road Not Taken 89

Letting Go 90

After the First There Is No Other 91

Good Night Moon 2005 92

Cat-Talk 93

The Birth of a Poem 94

About the Author 95

Spring

Success

I ripened in my spiky spring-green shell
from a white seed into a chocolate-brown chestnut
and with impatient, wild desire bulged against the confines of pregnancy,
until with a loud pang I burst the tough peels,
glistening with the creamy polish of birth,
anticipating wonders.

Then a child picked me up
and rubbing me between his moist palms
he spotted his own surprised reflection in my glossy surface.
At that moment my pride melted, smudging me with disappointment
for I no longer belonged
to myself alone.

Ute Carson

Bliss

Sweet nectar of babies,
sweaty down and creamy milk.
At the center of her world,
my baby is curled up like a raccoon in its tail,
eyes unfocused, mouth anchored to the source of endless nourishment.

I inhale the soothing, lulling scents.
The wounds we will inflict on each other some day,
not from malice nor bad intentions
but from seeing the world through different lenses,
are still hidden from awareness
by boundless contentment.

First Arrival

For Caitlin

When you were born
the sun and the moon stood at attention!
And because it was Christmas
I believed that the Star of David had halted over our house.

My happiness could not keep you from
seeking fulfillment beyond my dreams,
soaring beyond my fondest expectations.
But like a gong long ended,
its echo still reverberating for all to hear,
so will my joy at your arrival
forever resonate in the recesses of my fluttering heart.

Ute Carson

Our Time

For Claudia

At the sun's hour my heart swells with happiness
at your smiles, tiny first wrinkles crossing your smooth baby face.
Then it's moon time
and the grandfather clock on the mantle
strikes 2 or 3, the hour of solemn sleep.
I nurse and rock, rock and nurse,
hum and rock, rock and hum
as the house is hushed into silence,
broken only by your Dad's slight snoring,
my mother's regretful sighs,
your sister's angelic breathing.

I continue to hum as softly as a buzzing fly
so as not to disturb the soothing spirits' nightly watch.
I am reluctant to place you back into your crib,
because this is our hour, our dream time,
when I weave my contentment into your slurps and burps,
infusing my good wishes into your life to come.

Expectations

In the theatre the lights go down,
and as the curtain lifts I anticipate wonders.
But you say the brave lion roars in fake fur
and with a good wash the clown's mascara runs.
I thought that because I feel, you should feel,
because I need, you should need,
but we sit beside each other
and gaze in different directions.

Ute Carson

Mother Love

I do not cluck like a fretful hen,
nor are my feathers ruffled
when a fledgling leaves the nest.
I am more like a Scottish sheepdog,
ever watchful,
circling, circling,
mindful that none of her charges,
distracted by spring's fragrances,
strays through a thicket of golden bracken
onto the moors and the open hills.

Inner Light

The grape arbor is a cage
in which you pace, round and round,
stepping into old footprints,
eyes narrowed, scanning the soil.

Light frolics through dense foliage
dancing circles across your path,
then flitting to green vines above
skipping along the surface of slippery leaves
only to caper back down
to tickle your ears.

Pebbles glisten up from the ground for guidance
as you diligently search for something invisible.
I am a sunbeam
trying to catch your attention
but your concentration never wavers,
you never look up.

Ute Carson

Birthday Omen

The wonder of a snail's belly
flattened against the rain-spattered window,
contracting, then stretching forward along the wet surface,
confident, feelers like flexible reeds,
eyes glistening pinpricks,
its shell-house a full-blown parachute in easy reach,
only its soft underside exposed, at risk.
How does a snail balance its perception
between the desire for exploration and the need for protection?

I watch from inside,
it's my birthday!
I too am vulnerable
as I tap old memories,
and turn into a child again,
shivering with excitement, a sense of wonder,
impatiently anticipating visitors and gifts.
And I long with a quivering heart
to become the center of the world again
as I was so many years ago.

Mother's Day

When I was a child
my mother clutched me to her like a purse
containing all her valued belongings.
I tried to escape like a genie
squeezing through lacerated fabric, frayed seams.
But her needs always pulled me back
with the force of a magnet.
Then war came, I was older
and soldiers pursued us with hot raging breath.
Turning her body inside-out
my mother made me a pouch
and hid me in it like a baby kangaroo.
She was beaten and trampled,
I was saved.

Ute Carson

Gratitude

For Cecile

There is a knock
and my heart leaps like a startled frog.
Through the mist-covered evening
your soft footfalls approach, cat-like bounces.

With the rising coolness of the moist grass
I sense your fragrance_
and am reminded of the beginning
when you burst forth from my womb, singing.

Transformation

Pain is fire, electricity, loneliness,
being born from a cold womb,
skull glistening through translucent skin,
tenacious emotional cobwebs spiraling inward,
feeling as if a camel has walked over you!

Only when life becomes more interesting than suffering
and surfaces with breathtaking suddenness
does the heart thaw,
soul's lesions mend,
cells, nerves, fibers spiraling outward,
as you rock back and forth
on the back of that long-necked, humped mammal
with silky spider threads in its furry ears,
source of life's delights,
wool, milk and meat.

Ute Carson

My Garden

Weeding and pruning are like a haircut.
I tell my flowers and plants they need thinning and trimming
for new life to displace dead foliage.

I pamper my vegetation with coffee grounds and horse manure
and in winter I cover the most sensitive growth
with plastic sheets and paper bags.

February began with balmy weather,
mossy carpets sprouted from under wilted grass
and the remains of rotted leaves.

I was away
when a late frost invaded the exposed landscape
and destroyed my greening kingdom.

Years ago, my mother had given me a dieffenbachia,
a delicate but resilient plant
which flourished under my protective care.

The morning after the frost
the fleshy black and emerald-striped leaves drooped.
Even the stems were sagging.

I pulled up a lifeless root.
How quickly everything can fail.
I shed a tear in sorrow.

Then I spotted a soft green stalk
balancing a tightly enclosed virginal crown
holding back its fragrance.

A daffodil! Herald of spring!
"I am here. Look at me."
I shed a tear for joy.

In Praise of My Mother's Womb

Velveteen blood-paneled room,
my first hide-out
where noises and emotions beyond the walls
reached me in whispered undulations
and the sound of my own heart pulsed in my ears.
In the water of creation
I lolled and played like a dolphin,
awash in amniotic pleasure.
For nine months I lived in this ocean of plenty
blowing bubbles of bliss
into the holy darkness
until one day
I was swept on cresting waves
onto the sun-baked shores of life,
a wondering alien on dry land.

Ute Carson

Lifeline

Birth,
a simple song,
a memory of creation,
a woman's wail the wind carries across the land.
Each birth bears cargo from past generations,
each baby is laden with treasured promises.

Maria called on the strength of the lioness
while giving birth under the fierce rule of an African sun.
Aenne, lavishing in featherbedding, herself severed
the umbilical cord of each of her five children.
Claribel slumbered under the influence of ether,
contractions coming and going on faraway shores.
And Gerda's birth pangs were drowned in tears of sorrow
at the death of her young husband.

Maybe life imposes its will on women,
uses them as vessels, cracked porcelain or sturdy clay.
Birth is women's work, heavy-footed or bone-tingling,
while men retreat, turtle-like,
or trail with helplessly hopeful hearts,
and children burst forth, spitfires or sweet cooing doves.

Under the high dome of possibilities
women dream multicolored birth stories
and conjure up spirits to help them through their labors.
And women own a lifeline,
a throbbing, twisting cord, swollen with energy
which carries all sustenance necessary for survival,
a soft rope of dependency
which must be snipped at delivery
as each baby is launched on life's current
and each woman's belly is crowned
with the mysterious coil of an ending and a new beginning.

Ode to My Thumb

As soon as I could unfurl my tiny fist
I went directly to you,
fluted silky flower stalk.
I sucked with all my infant might
until dampened with sweet saliva
you glistened as though oiled
and smelled of watercress and mint leaves,
my calming breath swirling around you,
cooling my appetite,
grasping contentment.

You were my earliest companion,
always at my beck and call,
providing comfort and self-reliance,
mimicking mother's breast.
To this day I remember your magical appeal
as my mouth makes the shape of
an appreciative "O".

Summer
Then
Fall

Driftwood

I laid our troubles like trophies at your feet.
Roll them over,
feel the smoothness of a stone,
finger the gnarls along a branch,
study the splinters in bones.
You thought they were driftwood
and with the ebbing of the tide
you sent them back to sea.

There I stood, a dam.
With a sigh, a clenched fist, a tear,
each piece slammed into the wall of pain
until I gathered the fragments in my drenched skirt
and took them home.
I spread the stones, branches and bones
upon my grassy carpet
and then waited for the sun to do the drying.

Ute Carson

Dread

My feet make stomping sounds in the dark
and I sing to the haunting ghosts of the past,
luring sweet dreams to bed.

Once my playmate flexed his biceps threateningly
and when I told him, "My Dad is as tall as a tree,"
he shriveled into a gnome.
Every time a lion roars with wild fervor,
I stick out my dragon tongue.

But I can't find a remedy for my nightmares of loss.
I rage and tremble that you might fall to fate.
Just yesterday, a gust of wind
ripped the ticket from my hand,
the lucky one I had just bought at the lottery.

No Change

I should know that palm trees don't bear apples,
and when I slice the coconut its creamy milk is not sour-sweet.
The juice is sticky and weaves a web
between my fingers, airy but tenacious like ivy.

You walk right through the webbing,
scraps of spider-lace cling to your face.
If Jesus could change water into wine
why can't I transform indifference into caring?

Ute Carson

Loneliness

During the brilliance of my seasons I waited for you
through sweltering nights
until my heart got so heavy
not even ardent desire could lift it up.

You appeared in small consolations
as glowing lightning bugs,
a rabbit dashing from scented shrubbery,
a frog concert lasting till the rosy dawn.

I stood in the noisy darkness
and longed until the leaves turned golden-brown.
Finally winter iced over all hope.
Only then did I pull my shawl tighter
and retreat to the fire inside,
each step an echo…alone, still all alone.

Me

I am all of these:
My childhood delights,
the youthful setbacks,
crippling trials and
transforming tribulations.
The voice of my younger years
still softly echoes,
and engrained habits cling
like skin to muscle and bone.

But over time I use my experience
to rub off worn-out layers of myself,
glancing down with satisfaction
at piles of discarded parched hide.

With the passing of each season
I squeeze from another tight cocoon
until with a quiver and a few tears
I emerge once more,
skin naked and exposed,
but New!

Ute Carson

You and Me

Our marriage
is like a tree.
Sap circulating
from earth-nourished roots
through tender marrow
to entwined branches
and sun-hungry leaves.
When a bough breaks,
the trunk remembers.

The Gift

The Woman carries loaves of steaming bread,
her arms a basket woven around them.
Then she stops and lets her load tumble into a flung-out apron.
She looks at me and breaks off a chunk,
a gift of soft, grainy dough
with a crusty rim, brown like an earthen vessel.

I hesitate, having hungered all morning instead
for a slice of a pulpy orange
its sweet juice coating my tongue
and its blossom-fragrance pleasing my nose.

The Woman has already turned
when I manage a belated thank-you.
Only the aroma of coal smoke and risen yeast
still hangs in the space between us.

Ute Carson

Imperfection

The sadness I feel for my failures is
that I tried so hard.
The list of my mishaps is endless
the small sins weigh me down.

Failing to see the distress signals
behind my lover's blinding smile,
or missing my mother's last heartbeat
because I fell asleep on my watch.

Once I lived in the paradise of a womb
frolicking like a fish.
Now long expelled,
I crawl into your arms, another cocoon,
begging that my tries, however frail and mismanaged,
will count against my shortcomings.

The Loner

Like a snail you emerge from your house to eat and mate,
then you retreat and darkness takes you in.
In winter you fortify your door with calcium spit,
all creature comforts live inside,
and only music echoes through the lone chambers of your heart.

Each year the rings of your house widen,
and the colors change from earthy-brown to golden-beige.
Then, during springtime when your feelers search for fresh shoots,
you call out, "Hey, I am in here. Stop! Stay!"
But the warm wind whistles past.

Ute Carson

Temptation

We now have agencies
that offer married couples safe affairs.
Stoking fresh fires in the loins?
Or leading down the path to Sodom and Gomorrah?

A breech of mutual trust might not be an unforgivable sin
but where is the body that once struggled
and dampened the flames of desire?
And where is the renewed spirit
which with cleansed conscience
emerged like a phoenix from the ashes?

There are worse transgressions than adultery
but I regret the loss
of a sense of truth
which once smoldered beneath all dishonesty.

Hit the Road

Leave the table
when no more love is served.
Even meager meals can nourish
but crumbs just increase hunger pangs.

When no more love is served
put on your walking shoes
and hit the road.
Someone out there
is surely waiting
to prepare your next meal.

Ute Carson

At the Funeral

Amidst the weeping
the baby still needs changing,
and five-year-old Bradley squeals
when his shoes squeak on the polished church floor.
After the wake, in the damp summer night,
the teenagers tease and giggle,
and Josh's loins ignite with a fire
like the one that consumed Grandpa's bones,
new suit, tie and all.
Like the floral wreath on the coffin
beginning and end are woven together,
still we long to be buds and blossoms
forgetting that eventually everything wilts.

Despair

It makes sense that when a child is born
somewhere a person dies,
keeping the balance
between life and death.

But when I read that a young girl, raped on the Turkish border,
carries her blind brother on her back
through rubble and rain
and then jumps with him from a sheer cliff
my sympathy for the sufferers loses its mooring
and flaps helplessly like a bird with a broken wing.

Like that bird
I struggle to fly up once more
to a branch, however brittle and fragile,
to try to catch sight of hope again.

Asking Forgiveness From the Dead

Life is a swift storm
blowing me across the years
like paper flurries on a busy street.
When I finally am able to pause
you are no longer alive
and guilt starts to suck me down to the bone.

My regrets are like whirlwinds in a thorn tree,
tossing me about until I am torn,
insatiable demons, wanting my tears.
How do I redeem myself?

I do not ask your forgiveness in the twilight zone of the spirits
but through the likeness of our hands, kneading, patching,
and the passing remarks of a kind neighbor pulling back a curtain,
"You look more like your mother every day."

Song of Autumn

I like the melody-shifting season best.
No longer the bursting greenness of summer,
not yet the resigned hibernation of winter.
It's fall that carries a magical tune,
when the sky embraces the earth
with one last ardent desire
and its desperate kisses
ignite nature's most fervent colors —
blood-red, flame-gold-orange.
My heart too sings
with the rhythm of creation,
still finding a home there
before its doors close
against the voices of the cold.

Ute Carson

Recognition

No mountain was too high,
each cliff a welcome challenge,
and ravines tickled my funny-bone.
Until one snowy winter day, climbing up a steep path
and rounding a corner with a huff
I spotted the lynx,
tufted ears, chunky haunches, ready to pounce.
My courage slithered into my boots,
and I stood still as an ice statue.
Her eyes held mine,
gleaming amber-honeyed, confident of her power,
pulling intuition right down from the sky,
mine squinting with panic.
Slowly, I breathed movement back into my limbs,
drawing up energy from the earth.
As my fear dissipated,
the fragrance between us changed,
I matched her strength with my knowledge.
As I respected her space, she acknowledged mine,
allowing me to retreat calmly,
while watching a magnificent beast
lick her paws, huge furry snowshoes.

Naturalization

For forty years an American writer
and still I dreamed in German,
kissed in German,
spat out curses in German,
and poems germinated only in my native tongue.

Until one day
out of the Anglo experience
a fresh shoot burrowed up to the light,
bursting into flower as an English poem,
thriving under an alien sun.

Rooted in the tradition of my childhood
each poem now takes nourishment from the present
and imperceptibly, I, the stranger
have become a born-again daughter,
sprouting new leaves in my adopted land.

Ute Carson

Dreams of Fame

I am not invited to the Hall of Fame
but stand instead outside,
peeking in through the frosted windowpane.
Multicolored talent flits by on fairy wings,
stroking magnificent book covers,
tenderly fingering pages of masterly achievement,
all smiles turned inward like indented navels.
I shiver and two mice scurry past my feet
as a flock of blackbirds flies off with my manuscript
and a flurry of pages flutters down.
When a hungry dog mistakes the binding of my book for a bone,
my hope crumples like brittle paper.
Then I blink and in that moment
my book pages become golden flower petals,
and eager publishers rush to gather them in.

Acceptance

We imprint the familiar,
the early faces, the childhood smells, sounds, trepidations.
Like a baby chick following
its mother hen's first clucking
we search for the root of our emotions all through life.
Not until one morning when your cinnamon toast
emits the fragrance of my grandmother's freshly baked rolls,
and your footsteps on the creaky stairs
echo the night murmurs of the house where I was born,
calming and lulling me to sleep,
does the old and familiar envelop the new
and you, son-in-law, are accepted.

Festival of Lights

"Star light, star bright
I wish I may, I wish I might …"
We hum our way through elves droves and space odysseys,
wander through wonderlands of sparkling fireworks
and submerge into fairytales bathed in dazzling lights.

Then we amble home,
the city limits a pale sky.
We cross a footbridge over a dark river,
the water below steaming like a cauldron,
from which smoke spirits lift their white arms
and shadows of live oaks dance like giant monsters
over the moonlit surface.

The night is alive with magic
and our imagination
transforms reality.
But look closely and you will see
that nature unceasingly unveils its secrets
in all its manifestations.

Mummum's Lebanese Meat Pies

Weathered hands in a South Texas town
kneading flour and water,
happiness and tears, elements of life.
Dexterous hands rolling out sheets thin as wafers,
onions weeping under the scrape of her knife,
salt and pepper sprinkled on minced meat.
"Make a T," her purposeful hands instruct,
"and fold the dough over the filling tight as a tamale."
Feathery touch brushing olive oil over pasty layers,
then into the oven goes the handmade offering.
Later, clad in potholders, grateful hands pull out the crisp tarts
smelling of Mother Earth, tentacles from the Middle East.
After the first bite, tasty rivulets run
from ancestors to great-grandchildren.
Lebanese Meat Pies for the young, old, her children and mine,
no child of Mummum's will ever go love-hungry.

Ute Carson

Sickbed

The night is whisper quiet
as my fever rages, sweat soaking into the crisp sheets,
fear dully throttling my throat
as my breathing labors.
I toss and turn with impatience at my helplessness.

When I am healthy I lick my old wounds,
parade insults like battle trophies
and retreat to past injuries as a justification for my ill-temper.

But during illness
I regress to the comforts of childhood
where on bygone shores
waves lapped over my squealing body
and my skin laughed with delight.

Morning comes with the racket of birds
and as I finally doze off
I suddenly savor the sweet taste of grandma's grated apples
and watch steam rise from my mother's potato dumplings
with hungry anticipation.

What Remains

On the death of a grandparent

Let's walk to your Tree of Life:
Deep roots, sturdy trunk,
a canopy of colorful wilting leaves.
Now I think of you as the wind blowing through and around the tree.
During passionate storms of youth
your face turned straight into the twisting gusts,
during adulthood the wind shifted, slowing the sap,
breathing steadily in and out through family and jobs,
your old age came as a sigh, the wind turning to a tender breeze,
until all is suddenly still.
Tranquil leaves on a spring morning,
the mystery of calmness.
But the air remains filled like a full-blown sail,
sweeping over falling leaves,
vibrating, singing along broken branches,
sending quivers like lightning into the tree trunk
while children, the next generations,
press their ears to the wrinkles in the bark
listening intently for your echo.

Ute Carson

Artifacts

We have moved the antique furniture to our new home,
reassembled head- and sideboards,
connected bases and tops with worn wooden pegs.
As I rub the oil into the 18th century cupboard
whispers escape from the hand-carvings
and moans seep from dry planks, warped and chapped.
Gently I polish the brass handles, the locks of intricate design
and where a corner is missing, an ornament broken off,
I carefully wipe my cloth over the ancient wounds.

A gilt-framed, yellowed photograph of my great-great-grandmother,
fan and petticoat swirling past pewter dishes on the shelves,
decorates the dark alcove of the sturdy breakfront.
And hidden among chiseled rosettes are an A and a P,
modest imprints of the cabinetmaker at St. Ivan,
a country castle near Prague.

Our six-year old grandson Nicholas gapes at the carved dragons
snarling from the drawer-faces.
Timidly his fingers touch a wood whorl,
then trace along the edge of a gouged groove.
I continue my work, smoothing, preserving.
Though I cannot see the previous owners' smiles
or watch the cabinetmaker at his craft,
I feel the presence of the past as in a dream,
laying hands on old wood and bygone lives.

Staying the Course

I gaze at the night sky
where silhouetted against the honey-colored face of the moon
a flock of snow geese swooshes past,
barely audible, like a breeze,
only their eerie calls interrupt the solitude of the late hour.

These birds mate for life,
rare in the animal kingdom.
We humans lack inborn fidelity.
Instead we struggle, break promises,
hot passion turns to hurtful indifference,
we come to know failure,
the consequence of bad choices,
and the nest we once lovingly built with a partner is abandoned.

I watch two snow geese gliding by,
side by side, immense wings spread like downy kites,
the tips of their feathers touching from time to time.
Do they recognize each other through gentle vibrations?
They tell of hazardous migrations,
distraction by other birds,
demands and duties, hunger and need.
Many don't survive. Still they bond.

Snow geese live by instinct
we humans must make choices,
we too lose feathers weathering storms,
but if we find a way through turbulence together
there is joy in smooth gliding.

Winter

White Feathers

As a child I believed that the bald eagle's head was bare
until I saw it crowned with white feathers,
symbols of pride and transformation.
Such contradiction!
Bald men are said to be virile into old age.
My eighty year-old grandfather,
his hairless scalp glistening with sweat beads of anticipation,
overruled my grandmother's coy reluctance—
"I'm not really in the mood tonight."

Then my grandmother died
still bearing an abundance of flowing white hair.
Observing my mother bathe and prepare her for burial,
I gasped. No pubic hair! Like a baby.
I hid my sadness at the sight.
Wanting to cover her nakedness,
I squeezed my eyes shut like clams
and fervently prayed, "A few white feathers…just a few?"

Ute Carson

Moving to the Condo

Why the heartache when comfort awaits us?
No more heaving of storm shutters,
no more sweat while mowing the lawn,
and no shortness of breath
since there won't be stairs.

But I will miss the knobbed rosebush, planted forty years ago
which still bears the occasional blossom.
I will miss the gravesite molehills covering cats, dogs, birds, even a turtle.
I will miss the bathroom where my water broke with each birthing.
And I will miss the ceiling in our bedroom
where painted stars twinkle down.

The years are sealed and secured in boxes.
One last stroll through house and garden.
I stub my toe on the broken-down sandbox
and something catches my eye. A wishbone?
When I kneel down, I spot an earth-worn wooden building block,
then spool back time
to when a child (which one?) sat creating her world,
one that was timeless, one that could never be moved.

The Old Woman

She walks home from the village leaning into the wind,
her gnarled body bent like a branch laden with snow.
In the evenings she watches from the tilting porch of her hut
as the mountain is veiled by the passing of the day's light.

As she rocks she sees
a lamb lose its footing and bounce like a ball down the slope,
its wooly legs catching the undergrowth,
baying as if slated for slaughter.

The bleating of helplessness
brings the old woman to her swollen feet.
Panting, she makes a path through the thorny thicket
until she cradles her newfound charge in her arms.

Then she descends,
each step taken lighter and freer than the last,
the stones no longer stumbling blocks,
her breath comes easily, determined.

And when she reaches the hut's safe haven,
the lamb struggling but alive,
years of hardship slide off her shoulders like worn out clothing.
As she straightens her crooked spine,
the old woman feels a new greenness sprouting all through her aching
bones.

Stirring

Your depression is like a haunted house
with all the windows facing in.
You wander through the labyrinth
getting caught by ghosts and spider webs,
while I stand at the entrance
with the keys of my experience
and cannot get in.

Your body is frozen in silence
dead to my touch,
your shoulders rounded into a bow
with muscles taught like strings.
Only tremors rippling across the backs of your hands
answer me.

Your shaggy dog,
coiled up like you on the soiled mattress,
his damp, trusting eyes
riveted on your every twitch
knows that sooner or later the spell will break
and he will be let out to run and play.
I too wait, sitting in the lone chair, thinking.

"Getting tired of me?" you ask.
When hours later I take my leave
and drive away, you stand in your front yard
lifting your right arm into the air,
a jerky gesture like a puppet.
I wave vigorously
as if wiping fog off the window,
until I round the next corner.

Once out of sight
I pull over,
slump over the steering wheel
and weep.

Tender Aging

Beneath the tough yellowed layers
the onion keeps its soft stripes
and my tears well up the deeper I peel.

Our confidence remains fragile, always subject to change,
our knowledge fragments as we acquire more,
and our feelings recoil with the first rain
as they did so many springs ago.

But like a dove
which coos its throaty calming sounds
indefatigably each sunrise,
we face the night horizon
with the lyrics of smiles.

Ute Carson

Permanence in Change

Your index finger traces the faint red threads of broken capillaries
down my thigh to my bony knee.
The tenderness in your fingertip
is like a reassuring smile.

At sixty-three, my third grandson's birth,
I did a headstand as a welcome.
Rounding down to a squat
I buried my head in my lap,
so dizzy was I from the effort and the joy.

When the morning glory opens its cup to the rising sun
a gentle closing at dusk is bound to follow.
And when I kiss your wilting lips,
without the impatience of fire,
they still flutter like candle flames.

How Careless We Were

How casually we treated our young loves,
put them on hold, played with them.
If we gambled and lost, so be it.
Now in old age,
every moment counts as if it were the last,
and we realize that "Forever" is that lucky penny
which flips off only once
from life's wheel of good fortune.

Ute Carson

Preparing For a Colonoscopy

Dutifully, I drink the concoction to cleanse my intestines,
and as shit runs from me like water
I am reminded that I am ninety percent water.

I feel like the wolf in Little Red Riding Hood,
the stones in his stomach dragging him down,
as the turbulence tunnels through my bellowing bowels.

I slither to the cool bathroom floor
where my lover catches me and,
wiping my blood-drained face,
smiles reassuringly: "Not everyone faints."

I glance at my muddied flesh,
smudged earthenware,
and wonder:
will this body ever again ignite desire?

I Will Still Miss the Yearning

When I am old, I will remember the first kiss
and how he smelled of damp grass and sour sweat.
I will travel along winding roads back to other men,
no longer caring if their hands were calloused or kind.
Sheets crumple under writhing bodies,
from joy, sorrow, age insomnia.
When I am old I will lie alone on my big lumpy bed
and roll my loves into a fragrant comforter,
leaving behind passion's gestures,
the close embraces, the provocative laughter.
It is the yearning I will miss,
a questioning glance,
a brushing touch,
a feathery flutter in my throat,
sensing in the softness of my belly
that desire lives on.

Ute Carson

Stones Concert 2005

I have no sympathy for that devil of a performer
who looks like a scarecrow blowing in the wind.
Instead I envy him
as he bounces off the stage
as if it were a trampoline.

We are contemporaries,
age mates, Mick and I,
and the electrifying music, the familiar old songs,
his enthusiastic waving and hooting
are bread and butter to me.

But why the letdown?
I can live with the beer smell.
It's the fragrance I miss
which once spread like wildfire
from one person's glowing joint to another.

In the Face of Death

Our mare is old, old,
her back swayed by 111 horse years, some would say.
She wheezes, hoofing along a grassy path
to the cemetery of equines, dogs and cats.
Under a cluster of pines she whiffs the morning mist,
flickering with memories of ancient instincts.
None of her companions join her in that place of departed spirits.

She pauses, dozes. A blood-red sunrise.
Up from the ground, she struggles once more this morning to her feet,
her rump buffeting the wind,
flanks heaving, swaying from side to side,
a weak heart pulsing against the remaining rhythms of her youth,
her ears perked at the sound of my voice,
bestowing calm.

Toward evening I feed her carrots and sing to her.
In the blink of an eye the lethal dose stops her,
gently her legs buckle,
the velveteen-brown irises dilate,
in eyes, ringed like an owl's,
wondering, questioning.
She slumps forward into prayer position,
deep obeisance to the earth,
her eyelashes wet with sweatdrops like tears.

A last breath, thin as fog,
an experience of awe?
The dividing line between visible and invisible realms,
there is always mystery in the face of death,
bitter even if accepted.
I am dazed by sadness.

The sky in the west is darkening,
the moon a perfect circle,
air moving in a great wind
making loud whooshing sounds,

rearranging my thoughts
and leading me through our years of shared adventures.
Thus am I released back to my everyday life
and must depart without a backward glance at my fallen companion.

Absent Fathers

I am chilled by memories of my fatherless youth
like strolling under the cold light of a winter moon.
Roll call in elementary school: "Father's Occupation?"
"Killed…" "Missing in action…"
"Disabled…"
"Gone…Gone…"
On lonely nights
I prayed for an ordinary life
made up of simple things,
everyday concerns,
common pleasures,
emotions rooted in relationships,
with just a few bearable hardships thrown in,
so my life could flow unimpeded
until the dawn of Three Score and Twenty,
running its course
with a sense of fulfillment.

Ute Carson

Photographs

The New York Times exhibits photographs
of twenty bedrooms of America's Young War Dead.
Engulfed in sadness
we see what the soldiers left behind,
pictures, trophies, flags, potted plants (a woman's room),
and beds of accumulated memories,
now covered with a cold sheen of emptiness
as the sun and moon pour in over quilts
stretched tightly under shadows of change,
edges neatly tucked in, orderly and crisp, like uniforms.

These photographs blur perception
as though snapped in the rain.
No more bodies
with the musky smells of restless adolescence,
no more songs of yearning,
no more whispers from rumpled sheets
where someone sought comfort from another.

Death has crept into these deserted rooms
where dreams once knew no bounds.
There is a pillow on one bed,
deep red as though dipped in wine
or in blood in a faraway country.
Against the soft layers of cloth
stuffed animals huddle close to each other,
security blankets, abandoned now,
mournfully licking their travel-weary paws
and trailing like fairy dust
back to childhoods of the once living.

Waiting

Before the operation I have flightless wings.
Fearful of the unknown,
angry at my body, my trusted ally,
for keeping secrets.
I combat my anxieties with the certainties of my life,
loves, satisfactions and a vision of Pegasus,
so that when the invasion ends
I can unfurl my wings and fly again.

Ute Carson

Holding on For Dear Life

Nothing like parents!
And when they leave me in charge
his world tumbles like his building blocks,
his mood turns pure dejection, "Mama, Dada."
My love engulfs him in waves,
holding, letting go, holding.
And as I press him to my chest,
his tears tender as new leaves,
he whips his legs in frustration,
his breath hissing behind his tongue,
and his arms hang on to my neck
as if it were a lifeline.
I relinquish myself
to this willful, needy wonder.

A Colorful Well-Worn Garment

My body is a beautifully spun tapestry
in which I live in wonder.
Moist and silky at birth, a tender web,
then designs singing out my youth
in emerald-green, fanciful orange.
As my maturity blows in the summer breeze
I fondly stroke and smooth out pleats,
noticing sparkling yellows and wild reds
in the new richly patterned cloth.
Through all my years I've taken good care of my wrap,
it can't be exchanged!
As the fabric thins with aging,
hems unravel, seams need stretching,
I knot gems of humble wisdom into the folds.
Until at the end of life (as with all things perishable)
I have to let go of my cherished garment
and with the scent of deep purple lilac dancing at my feet,
my body is transformed into earthdust and flowerseed,
or fire and ash floating with the lightness of birds
up into a sapphire-blue evening sky.

Loose Feathers

Beyond Us

In the gated community we can't see the beyond,
and the walls are blinders to where others live.
But every neighborhood has a flower girl
who died of cancer,
a young mother parading her baby,
a man with wandering eyes,
or an addict who wants to be held.

Like a blood-red ribbon humanity trails down each street
and the good neighbor might be a brother,
your son, the stranger who lives in your house.
What's out there is in us,
and if we break down the barricade,
the grass on the other side might really be greener.
Put on your traveling shoes,
you might even find treasures in a faraway land.

Ute Carson

Thank Goodness

How I haggle with God
 for loving the prodigal son best.
All that fuss over a lost sheep!
What about the steadfast one
grazing close to home?
Why is a rose's fragrance imbibed
only momentarily
while the sting of a thorn prick lingers on?
An unfaithful lover is pined for,
the loyal husband taken for granted.
Forgiveness is holy water for the slighted soul
but goodness is the sustaining bread of life.

Never Just Sex

Under the instinctual lid of procreation
the sexual cauldron seethes
with a myriad of warring needs.
There is communication through the body
when the sweet aroma of honeysuckle
hovers in the steamy spaces between.
In striking the right balance between tenderness and lust
the song of the senses can ring in harmony.
But sex can take on ominous disguises
camouflaging the compulsion to dominate, to break bonds,
and leave victims with deep red wounds.
Sex is eros and hate, life against thanatos,
snaked around each other like clinging vines,
each forever fighting for survival.

Ute Carson

Sweet Dreams For a Newborn

Since your fabulous arrival
my mind and body have shifted gears.
I no longer wake at the twitter of birds
but adjust my days and nights
to your nursing needs,
marveling that I can sustain your life completely.

Outside noises fade away
as I listen to your sounds.
Your cries signal hunger? Discomfort? Frustration?
Your heartbeat, pulsing two beats to my one,
your breaths, soft puffs, each one an affirmation.

In sleep your rosebud mouth
crinkles into the tiniest smile
and I wonder what you dream of.
Sweet milk? Warm skin?
Or the faint flutter of a hummingbird.

Put a Kiss on a Wish

My grandson Zachary pursues his fantasies as eagerly
as he builds his toy castles.
His honeyed voice incants:
"Let's ride on the back of a camel
through deserts all alone,
escaping danger like a lizard
by leaving parts of ourselves
behind on a stone.
Come with me
through dark forests
with a tiger as our guide,
let's fight pirates and smugglers,
in perfumed fields of lilies
we'll hide…"

His enthusiasm like pelting rain
while I fumble for my magic wand.
He falls silent, his blue eyes smile.
Then he murmurs,
"Let's put a kiss on our wishes."
Resolved. A true magician!
Anything is possible under the tender spell of a kiss.

Ute Carson

Only in My Dreams

Old age was an abstraction until I encountered it face-to-face.
My legs, agile as antelopes', couldn't possibly buckle
until one day they gave way on the attic stairs.
Wasn't it just yesterday that I piggybacked my grandkids?
Now my bones moan and my flesh has lost its splendor
as when a winter wind has shorn off foliage.
I used to handle problems with ease,
now I turn them over and over, obsessed as an addict.
Only in my dreams do I never grow old,
there, I am a child again, nimble as a cricket,
I kiss a boy beneath a shower of white cherry blossoms,
I cradle a baby in my arms, brimming with joy.
In my dreams I scramble, crab-like, back to bygone days
only to return to this day, even more attuned to the passing of time.
Whereupon I cobble together new tasks and heap them
upon my aging heart,
delaying the day when I must wrap my travel-weary body
in earth and leaves.

Butterfly

For Dylan

When I think of you
I see you full of grace,
born to beauty and perfection.
You slid from your womb-cocoon
with sweet murmurs,
gauzy wings encased, trembling.
Then sucked by a funnel of wind
you burst forth,
lustrous lepidoptera
translucent blue, starlit yellow and poppy red.

Ute Carson

Letztes Geleit — Final Escort

For everything there is a time and a season.
Downy snowflakes danced over my mother's casket
while the old fir tree branches moaned and shook
under the weight of their white burden
and grandchildren carried her up the steep icy path
to her earth-warm sleeping place.

A squirrel dropped nuts from the shelter of a tree fork
on my father-in-law's oak coffin,
thumping little wake-up calls
ringing through the ripe fall air.
It was high-noon when the cortege left the mortuary,
drove slowly down childhood streets,
past the park with the resting benches,
along the brook, gurgling with the delight of long-ago adventures.

From the familiar to the unknown
the mourners led like birds in formation,
accompanying the dead on their final journey.

Retrieval

For my mother

If wishing can move mountains,
I can awaken your spirit with incantation.
My skin prickly, my hair on end,
I seat you in a rickety armchair
and wrap you in a fleece blanket,
a keepsake from long ago.
Your wizened smile casts happiness
with shimmering nets of sunshine,
and I hold that image for meek hope to flicker.
But when I try to touch the silky skin of your hand,
your spirit departs like a fata morgana,
and only sweet memories
linger in the chilling emptiness.

Ute Carson

Wisdom

What do I know now that I wish I had known then?
That sex can be adventurous in old age,
that I was always more like my mother,
that I can tolerate wrinkles and full body bloom,
that I remain foolish in my dreams,
and that, when I look into your trusting eyes,
I realize, not surprised at all,
that devotion lies in the eye of the beholder.

Buddha Belly

Abdomen of my youth, sun-baked-golden,
flat like rolled-out dough,
my husband's five energetic fingers spanned across
my vulnerable flesh,
protecting solar plexus, locus of my power.

During pregnancies my belly rose, steaming,
his firm palm massaging indentations into the supple muscles,
my skin stretched tight like an apple peel,
my navel protruding, a pearl-like grape,
I exuded the fragrance of overripe fruit.
After each birth the billowing mound deflated,
withering into flaps, folds and wrinkles.

Over the years my mid-section took on padding
so that my husband needs both hands now
to make a heart-shape with his fingers over my navel.
On moody days I pine for my former trimness,
but on joyous ones I know that
in the depth of my velvety layers
grains of accumulated wisdom germinate,
already starting to smell of morning bread.

Ute Carson

Love's Embrace

I am a well-loved woman
by a well-loved man.
The music of his breath resonates on my skin,
his hands transform my flesh like a sorcerer's,
his fiery kisses sting,
my nipples become lightning rods to my womb,
and with solemn tenderness
his soft trunk
tunnels to my core.
The seams of my body
though frayed by age
stretch knowingly like a well-worn glove.
And when we are spent
we stay connected
like two cats with tails intertwined,
no longer knowing where love's embrace begins
or where it ends,
because I am a well-loved woman
by a well-loved man.

There But For the Grace of God Go I

Who placed the glittering crown of success on my head?
Why do my eyes glow like a jack-o-lantern with happiness from within?
Other peoples' sorrow brings meekness to the bow in my neck
and I am watchful like a hawk
lest hubris slink into my good deeds.
Each sunrise I raise my hands in joyful supplication
like the morning-glory in its daily ritual
opens its flower-heart to the golden sun.

Ute Carson

Ordinary Lives

I carve my initials into the rugged complexion of the old oak tree
And toss a message in a bottle to the sea,
hoping that someone will find it,
and answer.

Madness explodes brilliantly in Van Gogh's paintings
and Jimmy Hendrix's music is gripped by the ghost of obsession.
Men go to war to be honored with battle scars,
and Mother Teresa finds her salvation in sainthood.

But satisfaction dances in my granddaughter's tap steps
and in my grandson's voice
when he recites from the Torah without faltering.
The hottest tears are shed at their grandpa's funeral
and simplicity lacks neither depth nor meaning.
When at day's end hands reach for each other
we atone or complete ourselves
without the fanfare of grandeur.

The Road Not Taken

The road well-traveled
is not always paved with regret.
Maybe intuition, your lucky star,
urged you to follow a familiar path.

Secrets of the unknown
are strewn along the road not taken
where you might find moon dust
or rush to your doom.

As you curl up with a book in your brown leather chair
you feel grateful that the lure of curiosity
did not drive you from your home
and the warmth of contentment.

Ute Carson

Letting Go

Everything speaks to me!
Even the stain which I try to wipe away
keeps bleeding at the edges,
and the wound continues to cry out
because I keep picking at the scab.
I swing my ruby gem pendulum-fashion
over my throbbing heart,
hoping to exorcise a time-worn grudge,
so that she who hurt me once can be put to rest,
knowing that we both wear crowns of thorns.

After the First There Is No Other

After your first lover's lips
no others taste like chocolate.
And you only heed your baby's first calls
with the flitting joy of a hummingbird.
When you lose a dear one without knowing grief,
the emotional umbilical stretches to them but won't break.

When a soldier goes to war,
after the first fear there is only night-dread.
After the first death blame is laid on the other,
then numbness camouflages the warring mood.
When merciful Lethe drowns guilt,
a stranger is born
with familiar arms, mouth, eyes,
but an iced-over heart.

Ute Carson

Good Night Moon 2005

On this cold December night
the moon is full one final time,
rounded out in golden splendor,
cream-colored like lit smoked glass,
its reflection on the tranquil ocean surface
a large gilded porcelain platter
from which I am emotionally nourished
and physically strengthened.
As the moon waxes and wanes,
always constant in its presence,
I stare at the 5 on the digital clock
flashing, blinking, pulsing,
crimson, scarlet, burgundy,
soon to roll over to 6
only to reappear in good time.
And I feel a tactile longing
for all my loved ones past and present.
I send out an ardent wish
for moments of clarity and yearning
as apparent as the moon
about to bid the old year good night.

Cat-Talk

Humans mark territory with fences and communicate mainly with words.
Gray tiger-striped Patches, cat-watchman with notched ears,
sprays trees, flowers and house walls,
his perpendicular tail an exclamation mark against intruders.
But indoors he spares our French sofa stuffed with horse hair, and my
German feather bedding, even antique table and chair legs.
Panther-black Aladin, fierce warrior,
lays his trophy, a baby pigeon, at my doorstep,
his whiskers decorated with down and drops of blood,
then retracts his sharp weapons into soft padded washcloths,
and sprawls in a spot of sunlight on the oriental rug
where he spit-slicks his coat until it shines like aged mahogany.
Sleek orange-coated Easter, goddess of our feline household,
keeps time for us all.

Come 6 pm, the News Hour, she waits at the entrance to the TV room
where my lap welcomes her warm body,
more soothing than a hot water bottle.
Scrawny white-haired Tiny, queen of hearts,
snuggling against my mother's chest,
purring in unison with her labored breathing,
was present at her last breath while I had fallen asleep on my watch.
After my mother's body was removed Tiny jumped back into the sheets,
sniffed for familiar scents and curled up, awaiting my mother's return.

I am late preparing dinner.
Delicate Easter rubs her electric flanks against my calves,
"Hurry up! You'll miss the beginning. The weatherman is already on."

Ute Carson

The Birth of a Poem

Weighed down by thick layers of warm earth,
the seed hibernates through several seasons.
But when at last its green shoot pokes through the tough crust
it is determined to succeed
and nothing, not punishing rain or scalding sun,
can stop it from ripening into full bloom.

About the Author

A writer from youth, German-born Ute Carson's first story was published in 1977. Her story "The Fall" won the Grand Prize for Prose and was

published in the short story and poetry anthology, A Walk Through My Garden, Outrider Press, Chicago 2007. Her novel "Colt Tailing," was published in September 2004 and was a finalist for the Peter Taylor Book Award Prize for the Novel. Her second novel "In Transit" was published in 2008. Her poems have appeared in numerous journals and magazines here and abroad. Carson's poetry was featured on the televised Spoken Word Showcase 2009 and 2010, ChannelAustin, TX.

An Advanced Certified Clinical Hypnotist, Ute Carson resides in Austin, TX with her husband. They have three daughters, five grandchildren, two horses and a number of cats. Visit her website at www.utecarson.com.

CPSIA information can be obtained at www.ICGtesting.com
Printed in the USA
238036LV00001B/136/P